To: ....

From: ....

L•I•S•T•S F•O•R L•I•V•I•N•G

Inspiration for Every Season

LISTS FOR LIVING

Published in 2008 by Struik Christian Gifts
An imprint of Struik Christian Books
A division of New Holland Publishing (South Africa) (Pty) Ltd
(New Holland Publishing is a member of Avusa Ltd)
Cornelis Struik House
80 McKenzie Street
Cape Town 8001

Reg. No. 1971/009721/07

Project management and selection by Reinata Thirion
DTP design by Marthie Dumas
DTP by Tessa Fortuin
Cover design by Joleen Coetzee
Cover image by Gallo Images/Getty Images
Printed and bound by China Printing & Translation
Services, Ltd, Hong Kong

ISBN 978-1-4153-0365-8

www.struikchristianbooks.co.za

C·O·N·T·E·N·T·S

I·N·T·R·O·D·U·C·T·I·O·N

Add sparkle to an ordinary day with these suggestions for any season of the year – Joyful Summer; Reflective Autumn; the Restorative Winter and New Beginnings of Spring.

Lists for Living will help you make the most of all aspects of your life – friendships, fun, creativity, wardrobe, lifestyle, spirituality and much more. It contains suggestions to help you through trying times, ideas for fun things to do when you need inspiration and bright ideas when you can't think of any.

Never intended to provide comprehensive lists on the topics, it is meant to spark your imagination, jumpstart your creativity and bring some light-hearted moments into your day.

Browse the topics, enjoy the quotations, try some of the ideas, share some with your friends. And when you're done, it's your turn to come up with some imaginative lists of your own ...

S·U·M·M·E·R

There shall be
eternal summer in
the grateful heart.

– Celia Thaxter

LIVING LIFE PASSIONATELY

So whether you eat or drink or whatever you do, do it all for the glory of God.

– 1 Corinthians 10:31

- Don't set you life on 'automatic' – life is too short not to live with abandon
- Do something spontaneous and impulsive
- Wear a bright coloured dress or shirt to celebrate the goodness of life
- Learn a new skill
- Be passionate about your faith
- Conquer your fear of failure – do something you have never done before
- Do something extraordinary – decide to run a marathon, go on an overseas trip, climb Kilimanjaro, ride a giraffe
- Laugh a lot – find the humour in life
- Do something extravagant – give a huge batch of cookies to your child to take to boarding school; pick as many flowers as you have in your garden and deliver them to a friend

A THANKFUL HEART

The fear of the LORD leads to life: Then one rests content, untouched by trouble

– Proverbs 19:23

- Keep a 'gratitude journal'. Decide that for one week, you will not ask anything from God; instead, every evening write down five different things to be grateful for

- Take your time enjoying a cup of tea or coffee in your favourite chair

- Live in the present – make a point of consciously savouring the small, good things in life like the smile of a stranger, the warmth of the sun on your skin, the laughter of a child

- Remind yourself of what you do have when you start complaining about what you lack

POSITIVE THINGS TO STIR YOUR OPTIMISM

Optimism is the foundation of courage.

– Nicholas Murray Butler

- Think of one thing to look forward to every morning
- Get a pot plant or pet to look after
- Decide to compliment every person you deal with today – sincerely!
- Every evening think of one good thing that happened to you during the day
- Make a habit of noticing the beauty around you
- Find a 'motto for the week' and put it up where you can see it – remind yourself of it as often as possible
- Make a point of smiling often
- Read a motivational book
- Choose one negative word you want to remove from your vocabulary this month
- How do you want people to remember you? See yourself as that person – it will make it easier to become that person!
- Wear a brightly coloured shirt to work today

APPRECIATE YOUR FRIENDS

Just as lotions and fragrance
give sensual delight, a sweet
friendship refreshes the soul.

– Proverbs 27:9 (The Message)

- Tell her that you appreciate her – too often we leave these things unsaid

- Buy a small, thoughtful gift for a friend when it is not her birthday

- Send a card to a friend, making mention of something that you especially appreciate about her

- Take a friend out for coffee to let her know that she is special

- Make an 'I appreciate you because' jar: Fill a nice jar with slips of different coloured paper, each with a reason you appreciate her

NURTURING YOUR FRIENDSHIPS

A friend loves at all times,
and a brother is born for adversity.

– Proverbs 17:17

- Be the kind of friend you want to have

- Be your friends' cheerleader – celebrate their success with them

- Respect your friends – what you think of them on the inside, will show on the outside

- Accept your friends with all their faults, quirks and issues – don't try to 'fix' them

- Listen! Show them that what they have to say is important to you

- Keep things your friends tell you confidential

- Tell others only good things about your friends

- Call your friends for no specific reason, except to let them know you care

BREAKFAST IDEAS
FOR BUSY PEOPLE

All happiness depends on a leisurely breakfast.

— John Günter

- A few pieces of fruit with a handful of nuts and sun-flower seeds
- Half a grapefruit (you could also drizzle honey over it)
- Instant Oatmeal with a banana
- Mashed avocado on whole-wheat toast – season with a sprinkling of salt and lemon juice
- Breakfast smoothie – set out everything you need the night before
- Yogurt with nuts and muesli
- Boiled or scrambled egg on whole-wheat toast – you can boil the egg the night before
- Buy some muffins to wrap and freeze individually – just take out what you need the night before

A RECIPE FOR LOVING OTHERS

- Love never gives up
- Love cares more for others than for self
- Love doesn't want what it doesn't have
- Love doesn't strut
- Doesn't have a swelled head
- Doesn't force itself on others
- Isn't always 'me first'
- Doesn't fly off the handle
- Doesn't keep score of the sins of others
- Doesn't revel when others grovel
- Takes pleasure in the flowering of truth
- Puts up with anything
- Trusts God always
- Always looks for the best
- Never looks back
- But keeps going to the end

– 1 Corinthians 13:1-7 (The Message)

PLACES TO GO

Go out there and do something remarkable.
– Wendy Wasserstein

- ❧ Visit an observatory on a star-filled night
- ❧ Ride your nearest roller coaster
- ❧ Be a tourist in your own town – ask around or read up on places you have not seen of visited yet and go there
- ❧ Go to a play, ballet or orchestra
- ❧ Spend the day at a fair and street market
- ❧ Visit an art museum
- ❧ Spend a morning in a near-by nature reserve
- ❧ Visit a farm in your area
- ❧ Gather a group of friends and have appetizers in one restaurant, the main course at another, dessert and coffee at yet another coffee shop

BE ADVENTUROUS!

An adventure is only an inconvenience rightly considered. An inconvenience is only an adventure wrongly considered.

– GK Chesterton

- Ride a horse on the beach
- Go four-wheel driving
- Learn how to use a compass, then go and use your skills
- Ride a rollercoaster
- Try cliff jumping or rock climbing
- Go mountain biking with some friends
- Sample some foreign food – try something different like Korean, Thai, Greek or French food, something you've never had before

- Canoe at dawn
- Wake up in the morning, take a picnic lunch, get in your car and see where the day takes you
- Randomly choose a hairstylist from your yellow pages, go to them and give them complete freedom to do to you whatever they want
- Take to the air – paragliding, hang gliding or a hot-air balloon ride
- Learn how to scuba dive
- Go on a night hike

LIVE JOYFULLY

Our mouths were filled with laughter,
our tongues with songs of joy … The LORD has done
great things for us, and we are filled with joy.

– Psalm 126:2–3

- Celebrate small victories and daily blessings
- Feeling forgiven brings joy – remind yourself that you are forgiven by God, and thank Him for his love and forgiveness whenever you feel heavy-hearted
- Bring joy to someone else with a small gift or act of kindness
- Trust God to surprise you with joy today
- Make a 'praise list' of all the gifts God has given you: the birds that sing as you awake, a friend's hug, a compliment or sunshine after a rainy day
- Forgiving others builds our joy – make sure that you don't hold grudges
- Write out ten things that make you happy – then do one of them
- Throw a party for no reason at all
- Exercise – a de-stressed body is more receptive to joy

FUN THINGS TO DO

Live life so completely that when death comes to you like a thief in the night, there will be nothing left for him to steal.

- Listen to music that you don't normally listen to
- Cook popcorn with the lid off
- Picnic on the beach
- Rent your favourite movie, make some popcorn and enjoy it!
- Make an entertaining phone answering-machine message
- Go and test drive that car you've always wanted
- Join a pottery class
- Look at the stars – if you have a telescope, even better!
- Attend a craft workshop
- Take a book with you and spend some time reading in your favourite coffee shop
- Take a moonlight bike ride

BE MORE CONFIDENT

But blessed is the man
who trusts in the LORD,
whose confidence is in him.

– Jeremiah 17:7

- Understand who you are in God' eyes
- Don't compare yourself with other people
- Accept compliments gracefully
- Don't think about yourself too much. Try not to focus negatively on how you come across or how others may perceive you; instead focus more on making other people happy
- Take a public speaking course

- Surround yourself with nurturing friends

- Be positive, even if you don't feel positive

- Help others. When you know you're kind to the people around you, and are making a positive difference in other people's lives it will boost your self-confidence

- Prepare thoroughly for any task so that you can be sure you are ready

- Act as if you were self-confident – you will feel more confident

- Focus on your achievements rather than your failures

- Always smile and stand up straight

- Take action. It is surprising how powerful the simple step of taking an action can be. It could be something as simple as tackling a task that you have been pro-crastinating, such as writing a letter or tidying up that corner of the garage that has been out of control for the last several months

SMALL STEPS TO HEALTHY LIVING

*I hope that you are as strong in body,
as I know you are in spirit.*

– 3 John 2, CEV

- Go to bed early tonight
- Choose one physical activity to start doing
- Make one positive change in your eating habits each week
- Treat your body as the temple of the Holy Spirit (1 Cor 6:19)
- Listen to your body's needs
- Make sure you get all your vitamins – take a good multi-vitamin if you need it

SUMMER FITNESS

Health and cheerfulness naturally beget each other.
– Joseph Addison

- Play frisbee with your children or friends
- Have a picnic on top of a mountain
- Rowing is great exercise and great fun
- Mow the lawn with a push mower
- Walk during your lunch hour
- Yard work can burn many extra kilojoules
- Swim with your kids
- Walk the beach instead of sunbathing
- Go hiking – explore the parks and forests in your area
- Take up jogging

LIVING ONE DAY AT A TIME

One day at a time – this is enough.
Do not look back and grieve over the past for
it is gone; and do not be troubled about the future,
for it has not yet come. Live in the present, and
make it so beautiful it will be worth remembering.

- Just for today … I will try to live through this day only, and not tackle my whole life problem at once. I can do something for 12 hours that would appal me if I had to keep it up for a lifetime

- Just for today … I will be happy. This assumes to be true what Abraham Lincoln said, that, 'Most folks are as happy as they make up their minds to be'

- Just for today … I will adjust myself to what is, and not try to adjust everything to my own desires. I will take my 'luck' as it comes, and fit myself to it

- Just for today … I will try to strengthen my mind. I will study. I will learn something useful. I will not be a mental loafer. I will read something that requires thought and concentration

- Just for today … I will exercise my soul in three ways: I will do somebody a good turn and not get found out; if anybody knows of it, it will not count. I will do at least two things I don't want to do – just for exercise

I will not show anyone that my feelings are hurt:
they may be hurt, but today I will not show it

- Just for today ... I will be agreeable. I will look as well
  as I can, dress becomingly, talk low, act courteously,
  criticise not one bit, not find fault with anything, and
  not try to improve or regulate anybody except myself

- Just for today ... I will have a programme. I may not
  follow it exactly but I will have it. I will save myself
  from two pests: hurry and indecision

- Just for today ... I will have a quiet half hour all by
  myself, and relax. During this half hour, some time,
  I will try to get a better perspective of my life

- Just for today ... I will be unafraid. Especially, I will not
  be afraid to enjoy what is beautiful, and to believe that
  as I give to the world, so the world will give to me

GREAT IDEAS FOR SUMMER GIFTS

Giving frees us from the familiar territory of our own needs by opening our mind to the unexplained worlds occupied by the needs of others.

– Barbara Bush

- Give a potted plant in a container with a difference – an old coffee pot, brightly painted bucket or tin can
- Find fun-shaped silicone ice cube containers
- Hand paint a set of glasses
- Give a rose bush to a friend. Choose the rose according to her personality – maybe there's one that has her name
- Find or paint a brightly-coloured photo frame and add a picture of your friend and you
- Pack a picnic basket with a variety of goodies to enjoy
- Select a hurricane lamp, pretty lantern or candle holders that can be used outside
- Find seeds for different herbs and package it together with a pot and some soil to plant it in
- Coasters, placemats or serviettes in bright summer colours

RANDOM ACTS OF KINDNESS

'I tell you the truth, whatever you did for one of the least of these brothers of mine, you did for me'

– Matthew 25:40

- Pay for yourself as well as the car behind you next time you go through a toll gate

- Look for things to compliment and acknowledge in someone today. Do it from a sincere and caring heart

- Clean the yard of an elderly or injured homeowner

- Make get-well cards for patients in a children's hospital

- Pass the novels you have bought and read on to someone else to enjoy

- Bake pancakes or cookies to take to the attendants and shop assistants at you closest petrol station or corner café

RELAX WITH
A GOOD BOOK ...

Books are the quietest and most constant of friends; they are the most accessible and wisest of counsellors, and the most patient of teachers.

– Charles W Eliot

Make some time to read. Some classics to choose from are:

- *Pride and Prejudice* – Jane Austen
- *Jane Eyre* – Charlotte Bronte
- *Wuthering Heights* – Emily Bronte
- *Alice in Wonderland* – Lewis Carroll

- *A Christmas Carol* – Charles Dickens
- *Great Expectations* – Charles Dickens
- *Oliver Twist* – Charles Dickens
- *The Count of Monte Cristo* – Alexandre Dumas
- *The Wind in the Willows* – Kenneth Grahame
- *Les Miserables* – Victor Hugo
- *The Lion, the Witch, and the Wardrobe* – CS Lewis
- *Anne of Green Gables* – Lucy Maud Montgomery
- *Lord of the Rings Trilogy* – JRR Tolkien
- *The Adventures of Tom Sawyer* – Mark Twain

DEVELOP A POSITIVE ATTITUDE

I can do everything through him
who gives me strength.

– Philippians 4:13

- ✍ When you wake up, choose to have a positive attitude during the day

- ✍ Picture yourself having a successful day

- ✍ Spend time with other positive people

- ✍ Steer clear of those who drag you down and always say negative things

- ✍ Be grateful for what you do have

- ✍ Always keep your sense of humour

- ✍ When you see the signs of a negative attitude or feelings creeping into your mind, stop yourself and focus on something positive or on possible solutions

- ✍ Create sticky notes with positive statements like, I can do it, I am capable, I have a purpose, etc and stick them up on your car dashboard, study table, personal diary, study room cupboard and dining places where you can see the message every day and night

SUMMER TIME
KIDS' ACTIVITIES

A three year old child is a being who gets almost as much fun out of a fifty-six dollar set of swings as it does out of finding a small green worm.

– Bill Vaughan

- ❧ Go hand pick fresh fruit – there is nothing like eating fresh strawberries or cherries out on a farm

- ❧ Go fishing

- ❧ Visit the zoo

- ❧ Start some type of collection – bugs, leaves, marbles of every colour and shape, coins or whatever interests them

- ❧ Go biking – pack a small backpack with water, snacks and drinks

- ❧ Visit a farmer's market to see all the vendors and fresh produce

BIBLE-READING IDEAS

*All Scripture is God-breathed and is useful
for teaching, rebuking, correcting and
training in righteousness ...*

– 2 Timothy 3:16

- ✒ Use a Bible-reading plan – read through the Bible in a year, the Gospels in a month, etc

- ✒ Keep a journal – write down daily what you feel God is saying to you through his Word

- ✒ Choose a topic or theme and make a study of it using a concordance

- ✒ Compare a passage in various translations of the Bible

- ✒ Listen to the Bible on CD while you drive to work

- ✒ Invest in a good study Bible

- ✒ Choose a character from the bible and make a study of his or her life

SUMMER GET-TOGETHERS

But friendship is precious, not only in the shade, but in the sunshine of life, and thanks to a benevolent arrangement the greater part of life is sunshine.

– Thomas Jefferson

- ❧ Pool parties are not restricted to children! Spend a relaxing afternoon around the pool with some friends while someone else looks after the children

- ❧ Arrange a lazy breakfast or brunch

- ❧ Plan an ice cream get-together – provide all sorts of toppings, sauces and sweets and let everyone create their own masterpiece

- ❧ Have a picnic on the beach

IN THE GARDEN

You can bury a lot of troubles digging in the dirt.

– Author Unknown

- Hang a bird feeder in your garden

- Paint the handles of your garden tools with bright colours so they are easily identifiable. The colours will also add some cheerfulness to your garden

- Place a little bench in a special corner in your garden. Let that be your prayer corner

- To protect your back, use a skateboard to sit on and roll along the sidewalk or garden path as you tend to your border plants

- Create a small herb garden to use in your food instead of dried herbs

- Get a swing – hang a swing on a strong branch and use it whenever you need to laugh, relax or connect with your inner child!

ACCESSORISE FOR SUMMER

If most of us are ashamed of shabby clothes and shoddy furniture, let us be more ashamed of shabby ideas and shoddy philosophies ...

– Albert Einstein

Spoil yourself with one or more of the following:

- A brightly-coloured string of beads
- A pair of stylish sunglasses to protect your eyes
- A broad-brimmed hat to keep your face in the shade
- A sarong with bright, bold motifs
- A practical beach bag – one with its own little mat to sit on is especially handy

SUMMER QUOTES

Christ is not only a remedy for your
weariness and trouble, but He will also give
you an abundance of the contrary, joy and delight.

— Jonathan Edwards

❧

Keep your face to the sunshine and
you cannot see the shadow.

— Helen Keller

❧

A life without love is like a year without summer.

— Swedish Proverb

❧

What a beautiful, sunny morning.
It makes you happy to be alive, doesn't it?
We can't let the sun outshine us!
We have to beam, too!

— Takayuki Ikkaku, Arisa Hosaka and Toshihiro

In summer, the song sings itself.

– William Carlos Williams

❧

What sunshine is to flowers, smiles are to
humanity. These are but trifles, to be sure;
but, scattered along life's pathway,
the good they do is inconceivable.

– Joseph Addison

❧

Kind words can be short and easy to speak,
but their echoes are truly endless.

– Mother Teresa

❧

PSALMS FOR SUMMER TIME

This is the day the LORD has made;
let us rejoice and be glad in it.

– Psalm 118:24

❧

Delight yourself in the LORD and
he will give you the desires of your heart.

– Psalm 37:4

❧

It was you who set all the boundaries of the earth;
you made both summer and winter.

–Psalm 74:17

You have filled my heart
with greater joy than
when their grain and
new wine abound.

– Psalm 4:7

For you make me glad by your deeds, O LORD;
I sing for joy at the works of your hands.

– Psalm 92:4

❧

My lips will shout for joy when I sing praise to
you— I, whom you have redeemed

– Psalm 71:23

❧

Then will I go to the altar of God, to God, my joy
and my delight. I will praise you with
the harp, O God, my God.

–Psalm 43:4

Love is to the heart what the summer is to the
farmer's year – it brings to harvest all
the loveliest flowers of the soul.

– Author Unknown

Youth is like spring,
an over praised season more
remarkable for biting winds
than genial breezes. Autumn
is the mellower season, and
what we lose in flowers we
more than gain in fruits.

– Samuel Butler

A•U•T•U•M•N

BEING YOURSELF

I praise you because I am fearfully and wonderfully made; your works are wonderful …

– Psalm 139:14

- List the things you like about yourself

- List those things you need to work on

- List your strengths – ask someone else if you are unsure

- List the things you are not good at

- Choose not to worry constantly about what others think of you

- Be open and honest – you don't need to be able to do everything or pretend to like something just because others do

- Relax! Learn to laugh at yourself

- Believe in yourself

- Accept yourself as God made you

- Buy one item of clothing that reflects your personality and wear it with confidence

ACCESSORIES FOR AUTUMN DAYS

I would rather be adorned by beauty of character than jewels. Jewels are the gift of fortune, while character comes from within.

– Titus Maccius Plautus

- A beautiful, unique hair clip or hair band
- A bulky handbag in your favourite colour
- A classic belt
- Shawls against the autumn chill, matching your wardrobe
- A fun, colourful make-up bag

AGING GRACEFULLY

Nobody grows old merely by living a number
of years. We grow old by deserting our ideals.
Years may wrinkle the skin, but to give
up enthusiasm wrinkles the soul.

– Samuel Ullman

- Accept the fact that you are getting older
- Widen your interests – fill your bookshelves with books on different things. Attend lectures, participate in volunteer activities or start a new hobby
- Be friendly
- Develop and maintain a strong social support network of family, friends and colleagues
- Make an active commitment to learning and growth
- Remain goal oriented – regardless of your age, still set one, five, ten and twenty-year goals
- Don't become more conservative than ever – age is an attitude

MANAGING YOUR TIME

*Teach us to number our days aright,
that we may gain a heart of wisdom.*

– Psalm 90:12

- ✔ Make a list of all the things that you need to get done and eliminate any non-essential items

- ✔ Arrange your tasks in order of importance and urgency

- ✔ Don't procrastinate. When you feel yourself putting a task off for yet another day, make a point of doing that task immediately

- ✔ Learn to say 'no'

- ✔ What tasks or chores can you delegate? Recruit your children to help with household chores, hire a gardener to maintain your lawn. Make a list and do it today

- ✔ Are you a 'morning person' or a 'night owl'? Find out when you're at your best and plan to tackle difficult projects at the times of day when you are most alert

SMALL DIET CHANGES THAT MAKE A BIG DIFFERENCE

One should eat to live, not live to eat

– Benjamin Franklin

- Use fat free milk over whole milk
- Eat only half of your dessert
- Avoid food portions larger than your fist
- Increase the fibre in your diet
- Swop your normal soft drink for the diet version
- Eat off smaller plates
- Choose fruit for dessert
- Grill fruits or vegetables
- Snack on fruits and vegetables
- Try brown rice or whole-wheat pasta
- Flavour foods with herbs, spices, and other low fat seasonings

GET EXERCISE
WITHOUT NOTICING

Lack of activity destroys the good condition of every human being, while movement and methodical physical exercise save it and preserve it.

– Plato

- Take stairs instead of the escalator
- Carry your groceries instead of pushing a cart
- Walk briskly in the mall
- Park further from the store and walk
- Do yard work
- Bicycle to the store instead of driving
- Walk to a co-worker's desk instead of e-mailing or calling them
- Walk instead of driving whenever you can
- Play 'catch' with your kids

SIMPLIFY YOUR LIFE

*Eliminate physical clutter. More importantly,
eliminate spiritual clutter.*

– DH Mondfleur

- De-clutter – devote a weekend to purging the stuff you don't want

- Simplify your wardrobe – get rid of anything you don't actually wear

- Create a simplicity statement. What do you want your simple life to look like? Write it out

- Clear your desk

- Create a simple weekly dinner menu – decide on a week's worth of simple dinners, set a specific dinner for each night of the week, go grocery shopping for the ingredients

- Have a place for everything, and always put it there when you have finished with it

- Make a 'Most Important Tasks' list each day – set just three very important things you want to accomplish each day

WHEN YOU ARE WORRIED

'So do not worry, saying, "What shall we eat?" or "What shall we drink?" or "What shall we wear?" For the pagans run after all these things, and your heavenly Father knows that you need them.'

– Matthew 6:31–32

- Share your worries with a friend and pray about it together
- Memorise the verse above, write it down and put it up where you will see it regularly
- Make a list of ten things to be thankful for
- Give your worries to God – see in your imagination how you give it to Him and leave it there
- Choose to trust God for today – say it out loud to Him when you wake up in the mornings
- Live one day at a time – thank God for his provision for TODAY

IDEAS FOR PRAISING GOD

Let everything that has breath praise the Lord.

– Psalm 150:6

- Arrange a praise evening with your friend – every person can bring a Psalm to read, a psalm they wrote or a song they want to play to praise God

- Spend one day not asking God for anything; praise and thank Him instead during the day and in your prayer time

- Join a Christian dance group, or dance before the Lord in private

- Make a study of God's attributes, and praise Him for who He is

- Play a praise CD on your way to work and sing along

CONTENTMENT

The fear of the LORD leads to life:
Then one rests content, untouched by trouble.

– Proverbs 19:23

- Slow down and enjoy every task. Pay attention, instead of thinking about other things

- Sprinkle simple pleasures throughout your day. Know what your simple pleasures are, and put a few of them in each day

- Make frugality an enjoyable thing – instead of delayed gratification, try enjoying life now while saving for later

- Be thankful for the basics: food, shelter, family, friends, a job. Make a list of all these things present in your life so that you can see how truly blessed you are

- Volunteer! Not only will you feel like a different person, but it will also put life in a new perspective

SERENITY

The LORD is my shepherd, I shall not be in want.
He makes me lie down in green pastures,
he leads me beside quiet waters ...

– Psalm 23:1-2

In the book *The Serenity Prayer* Trevor Hudson discusses 'Living one day at a time' as a step to greater inner calm. A practical way to do this is to make a habit of what he calls the 'nightly review':

- Make some time to be quiet for a few moments. Take a few deep breaths to settle down. Invite God to be with you and to shed light on the past day

- Ask God to bring to mind one moment of the day for which you are most grateful. The moment which gave you the most life. Or when you received or gave the most love. If you could recapture one moment, which would it be? Relive this moment. Breathe in again the gratitude you felt, and thank God for it

- Ask God to bring to mind the moment you are least grateful for. The moment which drained you of life. Or when you received and gave the least love. Reflect on what was said and done at that moment. Acknowledge your feelings. Refrain from judging yourself. Share these feelings with God and let God's love fill you again

REACHING OUT AS A FAMILY

Each of you should look not only to your
own interests, but also to the interests of others.

– Philippians 2:4

- Create a charity jar: invite children to share some of their allowance with others. Decide as a family where to contribute the contents

- Build food baskets and give them to a needy family – involve your children in selecting canned goods, fruit and other treats to include and deliver it together

- Bake cookies for your local police station or hospital staff

- Encourage the family to go through their closets for clothes they haven't worn in a while and allow them to select which clothes or toys they wish to donate

- Clean up an outdoor area near you – a park, roadside or campground. Pick up litter in any public area

- Share dinner with a new neighbour or one who is alone

GOOD READS –
CHRISTIAN CLASSICS

*The worth of a book is to be measured by
what you can carry away from it.*

– James Bryce

There are many books written on Christianity. Make time
to read some classics such as:

- *The Imitation of Christ* – Thomas a Kempis
- *Experiencing God* – Henry T Blackaby
- *The Cost of Discipleship* – Dietrich Bonhoeffer
- *Pilgrim's Progress* – John Bunyan
- *My Utmost for His Highest* – Oswald Chambers
- *Orthodoxy* – GK Chesterton
- *Prayer* – Richard Foster
- *Foxe's Book of Martyrs* – John Foxe
- *The Secret of Happiness* – Billy Graham
- *Hinds' Feet on High Places* – Hannah Hurnard

- *The Practice of the Presence of God* – Brother Lawrence
- *Mere Christianity* – CS Lewis
- *The Ragamuffin Gospel* – Brennan Manning
- *The Father Heart of God* – Floyd McClung
- *Absolute Surrender* – Andrew Murray
- *The Normal Christian Life* – Watchman Nee
- *Knowing God* – JI Packer
- *Desiring God* – John Piper
- *I Dared to Call Him Father* – Bilquis Sheikh
- *The Grace Awakening* – Charles Swindoll
- *How to Pray* – RA Torrey
- *The Pursuit of God* – AW Tozer
- *The Spirit of the Disciplines* – Dallas Willard
- *The Heavenly Man* – Brother Yun

KEEPING IN TOUCH

*What a wonderful thing is the mail,
capable of conveying across continents
a warm human hand-clasp.*

– Author Unknown

Keeping long-distance families close and connected takes work and determination but the rewards last a lifetime.

- Consider an extra cell phone contract for the free minutes – get the cheapest one available. It's a great way to have some extra talk-time available

- Keep some cards, envelopes and stamps handy to send quick notes to friends and family

- Before you read the paper or while you're drinking that first cup of coffee, send some personal e-mails to keep in touch

- Often special occasions arise for friends and you just can't be there in person to celebrate. Sending a small gift in the mail is a great way to show that you care and that you wish you could be there

- A picture is still worth more than a thousand words – photographs, e-mailed or sent by regular mail will help keep the relationship 'real'

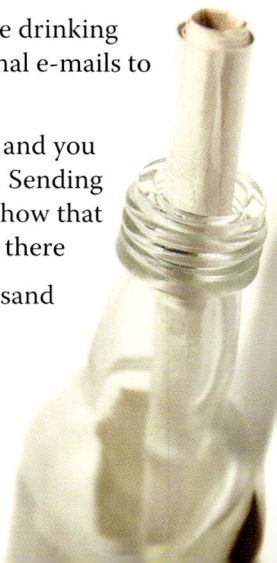

FUN AT WORK

*Find a job you like and you add
five days to every week.*

– H Jackson Browne

- Converse with coworkers on things not involving work
- Decorate a cake with 'Happy Tuesday' (or any other day of the week on it!) and take it to work
- Build friendships at work – get to know one of your colleagues better this week
- Decorate your office with fun posters
- Do things backwards. For example, when reading your e-mail, work from bottom to top. Sounds simple, but even little changes can be kind of fun
- Make your workspace feel more like home – have photos of your family and friends, a plant, a favourite mug, etc at the office

CHOICES

One's philosophy is not best expressed in words;
it is expressed in the choices one makes.

– Eleanor Roosevelt

The direction and quality of our lives are determined by our choices. What choices do you need to make? Don't wait too long!

I choose to:

- Forgive someone
- Have a positive attitude towards my children/husband/colleagues
- Colour my hair
- Eat healthier
- Start working out at the gym
- Love
- No longer let people walk all over me
- Be less critical of others
- Seek God's will for a certain situation

AUTUMN ACTIVITIES
FOR CHILDREN

You are worried about seeing him spend his early years in doing nothing. What! Is it nothing to be happy? Nothing to skip, play, and run around all day long? Never in his life will he be so busy again.

– Jean-Jacques Rousseau

- Build a 'survival shelter' from fallen branches and leaves
- Sleep in your survival shelter
- Record the temperature daily
- Collect dried wildflowers
- Press flowers; use them to decorate cards
- Set up a bird feeder outside the window – use a variety of seed to attract a variety of birds
- Check in your back garden for leaves to collect and stick in a scrapbook
- Do leaf printing by painting on to a leaf then pressing it to a page. Use leaves of different shapes

POSITIVE WORDS

*If anyone is never at fault in what he says,
he is a perfect man, able to keep his whole body in
check ... the tongue is a small part of the body,
but it makes great boasts.*

– James 3:2, 5

- When I want to criticise, I will think twice about what I want to say, and how to say it

- When I want to say something negative about someone, I will keep quiet

- Today I shall greet my unfriendly colleague with a smile

- Today I shall sincerely compliment at least three people

- I choose not to complain today

- Today I shall not say anything negative to myself, or about myself

- Today I shall be on the lookout for someone that needs encouragement

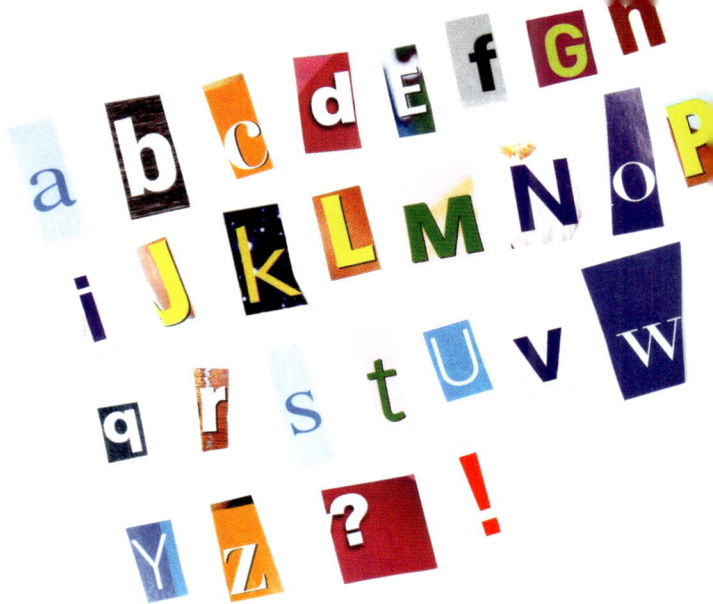

- I shall try and 'catch' my children doing something right – and tell them how I appreciate it

- Today I have no problems – only challenges, and that is how I will speak about it

- I want to tell someone close to me how much she means to me

- I am going to thank those who served me with a smile

- I shall thank God for every good thing I find in my day

TAKE A MOMENT
TO DE-STRESS

The time to relax is when you don't have time for it.
– Jim Goodwin

- Watch the clouds drift by
- Get a therapeutic massage
- Go a whole day without music, TV, newspapers or phone calls
- Drink coffee in the morning sunshine
- Feed the ducks at the park
- Get some flowers for yourself
- Unplug the phone and take a bubble bath
- Go outside and lie on the grass
- Grow something
- Pick a favourite place to watch the sunset or sunrise and go there often

HOSPITALITY

Do not forget to entertain strangers,
for by so doing some people have entertained
angels without knowing.

– Hebrews 13:2

- Invite someone with no family to share a meal with your family
- Invite a couple of friends over for tea and scones
- Offer to take care of a single mom's children to give her an afternoon or evening off
- Bake a batch of cookies or put together a hamper of fruit to share with your neighbours
- Offer to house a visiting missionary or Christian worker

ANYTIME SNACKS
AND TREATS

I doubt whether the world holds for anyone
a more soul-stirring surprise than the
first adventure with ice cream.

– Heywood Broun

- Chocolate-dipped strawberries (or any other fruit pieces)
- A mug of good hot chocolate topped with marshmal-lows
- A handful of almonds and dried fruit
- Apple slices with peanut butter
- Baked potato with low-fat cottage cheese
- Toasted pita bread triangles with hummus
- Pretzels with dip
- A scoop of your favourite ice-cream
- Bran muffins
- Air-popped popcorn
- Veggie sticks with low-fat dip or hummus
- Fruit yogurt sprinkled with a tablespoon of muesli

GIFT IDEAS FOR MOTHER'S DAY

*A hug is a great gift – one size fits all,
and it's easy to exchange.*

– Author Unknown

- A photo-album with pictures of you and your mum, siblings, special family occasions, etc. Leave some space to add some later too

- A voucher for a Facial treatment, massage of manicure

- Subscription to her favourite magazine

- Compile a personalised recipe book with the family's favourites –add photographs, personal messages and quotes, and leave a few blank pages to fIll up later on

- A hot-air balloon ride

- Put together a basket with her favourite body wash, bubble bath, body butter, etc

GIFT IDEAS FOR FATHER'S DAY

To give and then not feel that one has given is the very best of all ways of giving.

– Max Beerbohm

- A photo-album with pictures of you and your dad, siblings, special family occasions, etc. Leave some space to add some later too

- A subscription to a magazine

- Season tickets for rugby or cricket

- A special mug – a personalised mug would be even better – together with some gourmet blend coffee

- Put together a basket with his favourite goodies – biltong, sweets, wine, etc

- A novel version of a useful item such as corkscrew or bottle opener. Or any other useful gadget

THINGS TO DO WITH
FRIENDS IN AUTUMN

The only way to have a friend is to be one.
– Ralph Waldo Emerson

- Save up money and go with a friend on a 'pamper day'
- Have a chick-flick sleepover evening
- Attend an outdoor music event
- Have a photo day – take pictures of each other in various fun settings. Have prints made and spend another day putting them together in albums, frames or collages

QUOTES TO SAVOUR IN AUTUMN

No man can taste the fruits of autumn while he is delighting his scent with the flowers of spring.

– Samuel Johnson

Everyone must take time to sit and watch the leaves turn.

– Elizabeth Lawrence

Believe in yourself, your neighbours, your work, your ultimate attainment of more complete happiness. It is only the farmer who faithfully plants seeds in the Spring, who reaps a harvest in Autumn.

– Bertie Charles Forbes

Oh, would that my mind could let fall its dead ideas, as the tree does its withered leaves!

– Andre Gide

Unless a tree has borne blossoms in spring,
you will vainly look for fruit on it in autumn.

– Charles Hare and Augustus William Hare

Everyone thinks of changing the world, but no one
thinks of changing himself.

– Leo Tolstoy

Any change, even a change for the better, is always
accompanied by drawbacks and discomforts.

– Arnold Bennett

God grant me the serenity to accept the people
I cannot change, the courage to change the
one I can, and the wisdom to know it's me.

– Author Unknown

Life is change. Growth is optional. Choose wisely.

– Karen Kaiser Clark

VERSES TO ENCOURAGE
YOU IN AUTUMN

Jesus Christ is the same yesterday
and today and forever.

– Hebrews 13:8

❧

For the eyes of the LORD range throughout
the earth to strengthen those whose hearts
are fully committed to him.

– 2 Chronicles 16:9

❧

In a desert land he found him, in a barren and
howling waste. He shielded him and cared for him;
he guarded him as the apple of his eye, like an
eagle that stirs up its nest and hovers over
its young, that spreads its wings to catch
them and carries them on its pinions.

– Deuteronomy 32:10–11

Let us fix our eyes on Jesus, the author and perfecter
of our faith, who for the joy set before him endured
the cross, scorning its shame, and sat down at the
right hand of the throne of God.

– Hebrews 12:2

❧

'I have loved you with an everlasting love; I have
drawn you with loving-kindness.'

–Jeremiah 31:3

❧

Cast all your anxiety on him
because he cares for you.

– 1 Peter 5:7

❧

The Lord your God is with you, he is mighty
to save. He will take great delight in you,
he will quiet you with his love,
he will rejoice over you with singing.

– Zephaniah 3:17

W·I·N·T·E·R

In the depth of winter,
I finally learned that
within me there lay
an invincible summer.

— Albert Camus

DEALING WITH LONELINESS

The soul hardly ever realises it,
but whether he is a believer or not,
his loneliness is really a homesickness for God.

– Hubert van Zeller

- Avoid being 'ambushed' by loneliness – know when you tend to feel lonely and under which circumstances the loneliness gets too much. We cannot always avoid the circumstances, but if we are prepared the battle is halfway won already

- Do something you enjoy but never have time for

- Talk to God – tell Him how you feel

- Spoil yourself with a long bath

- Go for a walk or run somewhere where it is beautiful (but safe!)

- Read God's promises aloud to yourself

- Reach out to someone in need

PATIENCE WHEN YOU DON'T WANT TO WAIT

It is good to wait quietly for the salvation of the Lord.

– Lamentations 3:25-26

- Pray: tell God about your worry, your impatience and your fears

- Surrender: choose – more than once if necessary – to leave it in God's hands

- Spend time with positive people

- Keep a journal – write down what you are feeling, what you experience God saying to you, the promises He gives you

- Think back to those times you've been in a similar situation, and how you came through it

- Do: if there is something you should do – do it!

THEME BASKETS FOR CREATIVE GIVERS

*It isn't the size of the gift that matters,
but the size of the heart that gives it.*

– The Angels' Little Instruction Book

Buy a box or small basket, and put together a collection of little gifts by theme

- Ice Cream Sundae Gift Basket: sundae or ice cream bowls, spoons, an ice cream scoop, sprinkles, sweets like marshmallows, Astros or Smarties, ice cream sauces

- Wine Lover's Gift Basket: wine glasses, cheese and crackers, cork screw, bottle of wine

- Grandparent Gift Basket: children's artwork, gifts made by the kids, framed family pictures, candy, coffee, or tea, polar fleece lap blanket

- Gardener's Gift Basket: pretty gardening gloves, hand tools, vegetable and flower seeds, liquid fertilizer, kneeling pad, gardening book, subscription for a gardening magazine, plant markers, hand lotion

- Pasta Lover Gift Basket: package of gourmet pasta, tongs or pasta grabber, package of sun-dried tomatoes, extra-virgin olive oil, fancy olives, spices: oregano, basil, garlic powder, collection of your favourite pasta recipes hand-printed on recipe cards, pasta cookbook, jar of gourmet pasta sauce

- Pamper Yourself Gift Basket: candle or candles, bubble bath, pretty bath soaps, body spray, small box of chocolates, some decaf tea bags or coffee, body butter, a loofah or pretty bath sponge

- Baby Shower Gift Basket: baby powder, soap, lotions, pacifier, diaper pins, box of diapers, baby wipes, baby brush, bottles, small stuffed animal

- Kids Colouring Gift Basket: assorted papers, colouring books, crayons or colouring pencils, non-toxic markers, assorted stickers, paint box and brushes, safe scissors

LOVING YOURSELF

'Love your neighbor as yourself.'

– Matthew 22:39

- Forgive yourself for your mistakes

- Be kind to yourself – allow yourself to rest when you need it, to say 'no' when you have too much to do

- Deliberately stop yourself when you want to 'scold' yourself for something you have done

- Accept yourself for who you are – your looks, weaknesses, strengths, mistakes – God does, so you can too!

- Catch yourself when you want to put yourself down – replace it with positive thoughts about yourself

CELEBRATE
YOUR FEMININITY!

[Your beauty] ... should be that of your inner self,
the unfading beauty of a gentle and quiet spirit,
which is of great worth in God's sight.

– 1 Peter 3:4

- ✒ Relax in a bubble bath with candles and rose petals
- ✒ Write down five things that make you feel special
- ✒ Choose your favourite dress to wear to work and enjoy the way it makes you feel
- ✒ Spoil yourself with a bunch of flowers
- ✒ Make or buy something beautiful for your home
- ✒ Reflect on what God is busy doing in your life

SERVING THE HOMELESS IN WINTER

If you haven't any charity in your heart, you have the worst kind of heart trouble.

– Bob Hope

- Make extra sandwiches, or keep a bag of fruit such as bananas or apples in your car to give to children begging at traffic lights

- Collect spare blankets and clothes among friends and family and take them to a local shelter or organization involved with the homeless

- When shopping, buy a couple extra non-perishable food items and take them to a shelter

- Volunteer at a soup kitchen

- Clean out your closet and take the extra clothes to a local shelter or non-profit organization

LIVE ACCORDING TO YOUR CALLING

I urge you to live a life worthy
of the calling you have received.

– Ephesians 4:1

- Tell God that you say 'yes' to his calling today
- Choose one of the fruit of the Spirit in Galatians 5:22 and think of practical ways to live it out during the next two days
- Ask God to show you one specific thing He wants you to focus on today
- Think of a place where you can use your talents
- Write down how you can use your spiritual gifts to serve God
- Think of one specific way that you can bring glory to God during the day

STAY FIT DURING WINTER

*Lack of activity destroys the good condition
of every human being, while movement and
methodical physical exercise save it and preserve it.*

– Plato

- If you have stairs where you live or close by, spend 20 minutes at a time climbing up and down the stairs for a very intense and efficient workout

- Create a home gym. This doesn't have to be expensive. You can easily set-up a great workout routine with just a set of dumbbells, an exercise ball and a jump rope

- Get wet! Find a local indoor pool you can use. Try swimming, water aerobics or even just walking or running laps in the water

- Walk at an indoor location, like a mall. If you need extra motivation to get yourself to the mall, join a walking group. This will help you stay accountable to someone other than yourself

- Go ice-skating

CLOTHES AND ACCESSORIES FOR DREARY WINTER'S DAYS

Clothes and manners do not make the man; but, when he is made, they greatly improve his appearance.

– Henry Ward Beecher

- Be adventurous: get a hat that suits your personality and wear it often

- A cosy, cuddly scarf in bright colours will warm any cold winter's day

- Invest in a stylish, good quality coat

- Gloves in various colours will keep you warm and snug on cold mornings

- A pair of boots will go with most of your winter wardrobe and is an investment well worth making

HEALTHY OPTIONS
WHEN EATING OUT

*Good health and good sense are
two of life's greatest blessings.*

– Publilius Syrus

- Even before going out to eat, identify healthier choices at all kinds of restaurants

- Ask for salad dressing 'on the side'

- Choose a small or medium portion, or if main dishes are too big, choose an appetizer or a side dish instead

- Choose foods made with whole grains

- Look for items on the menu that are baked, grilled, dry-sautéed, broiled, poached or steamed

- When ordering pasta dishes, look for tomato-based sauces rather than cream-based sauces

- Order sandwiches with mustard rather than mayonnaise
- Take half of your meal home. The second half can serve as a second meal
- Ask for salsa with a baked potato instead of sour cream, butter or cheese
- Share a dessert with a friend
- Drink water, diet soda, or unsweetened tea or coffee instead of regular soda or alcoholic beverages

QUIET TIME IDEAS

He wakens me morning by morning,
wakens my ear to listen like one being taught.

– Isaiah 50:4

- ✐ Journaling – write down your questions to God, record what you think He is saying to you

- ✐ Take a walk through nature with God

- ✐ Set aside ten minutes in the middle of each day this week. Use the time to just connect with God and acknowledge his presence in your life

- ✐ Listen to some Gospel CDs – let God speak to you through the words of the songs

- ✐ Express your relationship with God in a creative way – write a poem about your love for Him, create a painting or drawing of how you see your relationship with Him

BABY STEPS TOWARDS 'LETTING GO'

But one thing I do: Forgetting what is behind and straining toward what is ahead, I press on toward the goal to win the prize for which God has called me heavenward in Christ Jesus.

– Philippians 3:13–14

- Sort through your clothes and donate the items you have not worn for the past two years to charity

- Write a one-sentence 'breath prayer' (e.g. 'Lord, help me live with open hands.') and pray it several times throughout the day

- Be flexible – consciously decide not to resist a sudden change in plans the next time it happens

- Plant a new kind of flower in your garden this season

- Do something totally new and adventurous

ENJOYING SOME 'ME-TIME'

Life lived amidst tension and busyness needs leisure. Leisure that recreates and renews ...

– C Neil Strait

- Treat yourself to chocolate – research has shown us that chocolate contains flavinoids that are associated with a decreased risk of heart problems!

- Master the art of daydreaming – lie on your back on the grass on a hot summer day and watch the clouds float by; let your thoughts drift to somewhere pleasant

- Get up earlier – set your alarm for fifteen minutes before you really need to get up. Then use that time to listen to the quiet, write in a journal, read, pray – do not use this time to get a head start on chores. Use this time for you

- Give yourself one night off per week – spend some time pursuing a hobby you love, reading a book, or reconnecting with a friend

- Take a walk on your lunch hour

- Make a date with yourself – mark at least one 'Me Time' date for this month

- Go to the book store or library

- Get a massage

- Grab a book and blanket, or even just your MP3, and go to a park

- Take a nap

- Find a recipe you like and make it

FORGIVENESS

Be kind and compassionate to one another,
forgiving each other, just as in
Christ God forgave you.

– Ephesians 4:32

❧ Remember that forgiveness is a choice we make, and
as we continually choose to forgive with our will; our
emotions will eventually catch up. But it starts with
the choice that we make to forgive

❧ Who do you need to forgive? Write down the name
of the person(s)

❧ Write the name and offence on a piece of paper

❧ Tell God about it one last time

❧ Make the decision to forgive the person

❧ Say it out loud: 'Because God has forgiven me,
I forgive (name). I will not hold this offence
against them any more

❧ Then, with emotion, tear up the paper

HANDLING DIFFICULT PEOPLE

A gentle answer turns away wrath,
but a harsh word stirs up anger.

– Proverbs 15:1

- Pray for them by name

- Accept that they might not change – accept them as they are

- Don't hold a grudge when they offend you – make the decision to forgive

- 'Kill them with kindness' – no matter what they do or say, be kind to them

- Thank them; make them feel appreciated and valuable

- Seek to understand their point of view, the issues that are real to them, their fears and insecurities

IDEAS FOR SCRAP-BOOKING

*Just as pieces stitched together in a quilt warm
our bodies, scrapbooks bind together
memories to warm our hearts.*

– Author Unknown

- Baby Scrapbook: You can record your baby's first step, write down the first word and preserve every precious memory

- Family Scrapbook: Help you and your children to remember what life was like for them growing up

- Mom or Dad Scrapbook: A scrapbook showing how much you appreciate them as the perfect gift for Mother's Day or Father's Day

- Engagement Scrapbook: Write the story of your relationship – include how you met, highlights, special moments, humorous incidents, etc

- Friendship Scrapbook: Preserve the special memories of your friendships; the fun you had, memorable moments and things you did together

- Birthday Scrapbook: Make a special scrapbook for a child on their eighteenth or twenty-first birthday

WINTER WARMTH – TIPS TO STAY SNUG AND WARM

Winter is the season in which people try to keep the house as warm as it was in the summer, when they complained about the heat.

– Anonymous

- Use an electric blanket or microwavable bean/rice bags
- Bundle up with long underwear, sweaters, hats, scarves, gloves and warm shoes
- Use rugs on bare floors
- Close unused rooms
- Keep moving – a little exercise will help keep you warm even if it's indoors
- Wearing several layers of clothing keeps you warmer than one thick layer
- A mug of hot soup, tea or hot chocolate will do wonders to keep you warm
- If you have a fireplace – make use of it! Spend some family time in front of a cozy fire

PREVENTING THOSE COLDS!

The greatest wealth is health.

– Virgil

- Avoid coming into contact with people who have colds, if possible

- Don't touch your face – It is common for the cold or flu virus to enter the body through the eyes, nose or mouth

- Avoid crowded, stuffy atmospheres where the risk of contracting the cold virus is much greater

- Wash hands thoroughly and frequently, especially after blowing your nose

- Keep rooms well ventilated at all times, and get out and get some fresh air

- Drink plenty of fluids – water flushes your system, washing out the germs as it re-hydrates you

- Eating a balanced, healthy diet including foods rich in Vitamin C and Zinc will help keep your immune system strong and allow your body to fight viruses better

- Cut alcohol consumption – alcohol dehydrates the body and leaves you more susceptible to colds

- Sneeze or cough into a tissue and then throw the tissue away

- Get plenty of rest or sleep to help strengthen your immune system

- Be sure that each member of your household uses separate drinking cups and towels

- Exercise helps boost the body's natural ability to fight viruses a couple of different ways

- Don't smoke – people who smoke are more likely to catch colds than people who don't

SAVING MONEY ON GROCERIES

If you would be wealthy, think of saving as well as getting.

– Benjamin Franklin

- Always shop with a list and stick to that list — don't buy anything that's not on there

- Plan out a weekly menu. This is the best way to ensure that your list is complete. Be sure to plan a leftovers night!

- Don't go shopping when you're hungry

- Have a budget – know exactly how much you can spend and try your best to stick within that limit

- Make a pantry checklist. Make a checklist of everything you normally stock in your pantry. Keep it posted on the pantry and make a note when you need to stock up again

- Keep your receipts, then enter into a spreadsheet. This will be your price list. Use it so you know when bulk or sale items are a good deal. It's also a great way to comparison shop between stores

- Cut back on meat. Meat is expensive. Plan vegetarian meals several times a week (e.g. pasta dishes)

- Cook a lot, then freeze. Plan to cook a big amount of food and freeze it for multiple dinners

- Look for specials. But don't buy them unless they're things you always use

- Try the store brands, especially if it's an ingredient in a dish where you can't taste the quality of that individual ingredient

- Cut back on your 'one-item' trips. They waste gas, and almost inevitably, you buy more than that one item

- Sale items can be a great deal. If it's an item you normally use, buy a bunch of them

- Don't waste leftovers. Have a list on your fridge of what leftovers are in there, so you don't forget about them. Plan a leftover night or two, so you're sure to eat them all

- Don't buy junk food (or buy as little as possible)

ENTERTAINING CHILDREN IN WINTER

There are no seven wonders of the world in the eyes of a child. There are seven million.

– Walt Streightiff

- Make a graph showing each day's high and low temperatures
- Go ice skating together
- Visit your local library and check out books on winter themes
- Use sheets or boxes to build a fort inside your house
- Bundle up in jackets and woolly hats, pull on some gumboots and go out and jump in puddles
- Have a movie day, pile the pillows on the couch and snuggle up under some blankets and watch your favourite movies
- Have a special afternoon tea with hot chocolate and your homemade treats
- Do a jigsaw puzzle or have a games tournament, winter days are great for a long Monopoly game
- Make a big pot of soup, let the kids grate the vegetables, measure and add the ingredients, stir it and then have it for dinner

BOARD GAMES TO PLAY

Life is a kind of Chess, with struggle,
competition, good and ill events

– Benjamin Franklin

- Monopoly
- Balderdash
- Pictionary
- Trivial Pursuit
- Cluedo
- Risk
- Snakes and Ladders
- The Ungame
- Scrabble
- Chess
- Chinese Chequers
- Create your own family board game
- Make some new, unique rules for existing board games

QUOTES TO WARM YOUR HEART IN WINTER

You aren't an accident or an incident ...
you are a gift to the world, a divine work of art,
signed by God ...You were deliberately planned,
specifically gifted and lovingly positioned on
this earth ... by the master Craftsman.

– Max Lucado

Only with winter-patience can we bring
the deep-desired, long awaited spring.

– Ann Morrow Lindbergh

Laughter is the sun that drives
winter from the human face.

– Victor Hugo

If we had no winter,
the spring would not be so pleasant;
if we did not sometimes taste of adversity,
prosperity would not be so welcome.

– Anne Bradstreet

One kind word can warm three winter months.

– Japanese Proverb

There is nothing, no circumstance, no trouble,
no testing that can ever touch me until. First of all,
it has come past God and past Christ. If it has
come that far, it has come with great purpose.

– Alan Redpath

Snowflakes are one of nature's most
fragile things, but just look what they
do when they stick together.

– Verna M Kelly

VERSES TO SUSTAIN YOU
THROUGH THE COLD OF WINTER

And we know that in all things God works
for the good of those who love him, who have
been called according to his purpose.

– Romans 8:28

God has said, 'Never will I leave you;
never will I forsake you.'

– Hebrews 13:5

He gives strength to the weary
and increases the power of the weak.
Even youths grow tired and weary,
and young men stumble and fall;
but those who hope in the LORD
will renew their strength.
They will soar on wings like eagles;
they will run and not grow weary,
they will walk and not be faint.

– Isaiah 40:29–31

... being confident of this,
that he who began a good work in
you will carry it on to completion
until the day of Christ Jesus.

– Philippians 1:6

❧

The Lord is my strength and my shield; my heart
trusts in him, and I am helped. My heart leaps for
joy and I will give thanks to him in song.

– Psalm 28:7

❧

'For I know the plans I have for you,'
declares the Lord,
'plans to prosper you and not to harm you,
plans to give you hope and a future.

– Jeremiah 29:11

❧

And my God will meet all your needs
according to his glorious riches in Christ Jesus.

– Philippians 4:19

Spring is nature's
way of saying,
'Let's party!'

– Robin Williams

S•P•R•I•N•G

SUPER-FAST DESERT IDEAS

My advice to you is not to inquire why or whither, but just enjoy your ice cream while it's on your plate.

– Thornton Wilder

- Frozen berries and icing sugar makes a great sauce – use as dip for finger biscuits or drizzle over ice cream or meringue nests
- Store-bought meringue nests filled with fresh fruit and cream
- Custard (and some orange zest or a bit of liqueur) with fresh seasonal fruit
- Fresh fruit salad and ice cream

- Bake squares of puff pastry and fill with cream, custard and fruit

- Core apples and stuff with dates. Bake in the microwave and serve with cream

- Whip cream and fold in some chocolate sandwich spread – use as a dip for fruits or meringue, or as filling for puff pastry

- Cut plums, peaches or pears in half, sprinkle with brown sugar and grill until soft. Serve with cream or custard

- Whip cream, fold in an equal amount of strawberry yogurt and serve with fresh strawberries or fruit salad

- Get creative with ice cream – use good vanilla ice cream and fold in fresh fruit, chocolate chips, crushed biscuits, liqueur, honey or whatever your imagination comes up with

HEALTHY LUNCH BOX IDEAS

Tell me what you eat, I'll tell you who you are.
– Anthelme Brillat-Savarin

- Choose interesting breads for sandwiches

- Pack a simple hunk of sun-dried tomato or olive bread with some thinly sliced cold meat or cheese to go with it

- Add interesting salad to all your sandwiches – rocket, shredded spring onions, finely chopped red peppers or bean sprouts

- Include fruit – try kiwi, cubed melon and blueberries or a handful of strawberries to keep it interesting

- Have some snacks handy: small packets of crisps, crackers with cheese, a biscuit, yogurt, scone or small chocolate bar

- Instead of bread, try little pots of pasta or rice salad, or pots of sliced salad veggies Make up a mix of chopped dried fruit, seeds and nuts

- Make a batch of muffins or scones and freeze them for packed lunches

- Pack some vegetables: a cooked corn cob, bean salad, carrot sticks, etc – include some dip in a little jar

- Collect small containers for dips, soups, salads and cut fruit

FITNESS IN SPRING

Exercise: you don't have time not to.

- Walk to the park – take the dog, or the children. Play on the swings; race each other to the slide
- Dance, dance, dance – turn on your favourite song and make up a dance routine
- Run or walk for charity – pick a walk/run geared toward families with kid entertainment and activities
- Rake the leaves – gardening uses almost every muscle in your body
- Skipping-rope – an old habit that's fun, trendy and family-friendly
- Post a note on the refrigerator each day as a reminder to take a walk
- Play frisbee with some friends
- Arrange a neighbourhood volleyball competition

WAYS TO STAY MOTIVATED TO REACH YOUR GOALS

Goals are dreams with deadlines.

– Diana Scharf Hunt

- Tell someone about your dream
- Create a poster that represents your dream
- Put it up where you can see it every day
- Plan a celebration for when you have reached your goal
- Keep a journal of your journey – record prayers answered regarding your dream

REACHING FOR YOUR DREAM

Everyone has dreams. But it is what you do with these dreams that are important. Dreams, once you make the decision to act on them, can become reality.

– Glynis Nunn

- What dreams do you have? Write it down

- Write down in a few sentences what it is going to take for you to achieve your goal. Plan to do it by a certain date

- Determine what skills you will need, or knowledge you must acquire in order to equip yourself, find out how/where you are going to acquire those skills

- Find someone to mentor you

- Identify the resources that you will need to achieve your goals. Now take each of those and start brainstorming on how you are going to acquire it

- Write down the next five small steps you need to take to achieve your dream. Set a date behind each one and tick it off once you have achieved it

RENEW YOUR MIND

Since you are precious and honoured in my sight, and because I love you, I will give men in exchange for you, and people in exchange for your life.

– Isaiah 43:4

- ✎ Write out a positive statement, based on the Bible, about yourself. Put it where you will see it during the day, and read it aloud to yourself (e.g. 'I am God's precious child; I am holy and dearly loved by Him,' based on Colossians 3:12)

- ✎ Ask God to make you aware of the times you say something negative about yourself (e.g. 'I am so stupid!' or 'I can't seem to do anything right.'). Turn it around into something positive

- ✎ Feed your mind with the truth of who you are by the books you read, the music you listen to and the people you associate with

- ✎ Read books on your identity in Christ, such as *Victory over Darkness* (Neil T Anderson), *The True Measure of a Women* (Lisa Bevere) or *Discovering Your Identity in Christ* (Charles F Stanley)

LOVING GOD

'Love the Lord your God with all your heart and with all your soul and with all your mind.' This is the first and greatest commandment …

– Matthew 22:37–39

- ❧ Spend time with your Heavenly Father
- ❧ Love others
- ❧ Obey Him when He asks you to do something
- ❧ Write your own love song to Him

GETTING ENOUGH REST

*He that can take rest is
greater than he that can take cities*

– Benjamin Franklin

- Get some exercise – regular exercise helps you sleep better

- Learn to say no – do what's most important, don't feel guilty if you do not manage everything else

- Share the load by getting family members to shoulder their load of chores

- Give to others in ways that boost your spirits

- Nap, if possible, if you're feeling tired or run down, even if only for ten minutes

- Eat healthy (balanced diet, lots of fruits and veggies), and avoid calorie-laden fast-foods

- Gently unwind by reading or listening to music for 30 minutes before going to bed

LIGHTEN YOUR LOAD – FOUR THINGS TO LET GO

'Come to me, all you who are weary and burdened, and I will give you rest.'

– Matthew 11:28

- ❧ Grudges: Let your grudges go. It is not easy, but ask the Lord to step in and heal your heart

- ❧ Fear: Lighten your load by trusting God more, one small step at a time

- ❧ Envy: Thank God for the talents He has given you – when you're thankful to God for all you have, right where you are, you stop fretting over others

- ❧ Worry: Refuse to let it put you in a state of helpless agitation. Trust God to take care of you

AWAKEN YOUR CREATIVITY

We have different gifts, according to the grace given us.

– Romans 12:6

- Surround yourself with beauty
- If you enjoy words, read poetry, a classic work of literature
- Spend time in nature – take the time to notice the beauty of a butterfly or the way the petals of a rose are placed
- Listen to music that inspires you
- Spend time enjoying works of art – paintings, sculptures, a beautifully designed home
- Look at the world through the eyes of a child

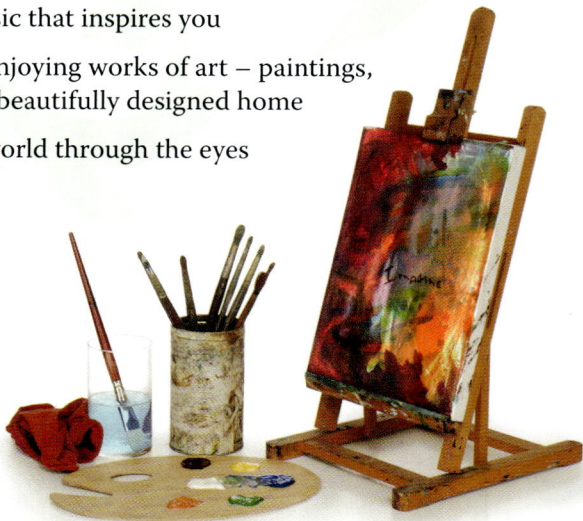

MEETING NEW PEOPLE

Two are better than one, because they have a good return for their work: If one falls down, his friend can help him up. But pity the man who falls and has no one to help him up!

– Ecclesiastes 4:9-10

- Invite a few close friends for a meal, asking them to each bring two of their friends along
- Make room in your heart for people that seemingly differ from you
- Join a sport club, cultural society or other activity outside of your normal routine
- Be willing and open to reach out to others

SUPER SMOOTHIES

*We are indeed much more than what we eat,
but what we eat can nevertheless help us
to be much more than what we are.*

– Adelle Davis

- Strawberry Orange Smoothie: fresh or frozen strawberries, orange juice and honey

- Chocolate Banana Smoothie –a ripe banana, chocolate syrup and milk

- Classic Blueberry Smoothie –fresh or frozen blueberries, frozen juice and yogurt

- Tropical Five Fruit Smoothie – banana, kiwi, mango, papaya and orange juice

- Creamsicle Smoothie – fresh cantaloupe melon, orange juice, vanilla extract and honey

- Berry Brainstorm Smoothie – frozen strawberries, blueberries, raspberries, juice and yogurt

- Pina Colada Smoothie – Made with pineapple, banana, coconut and milk

- Cherry Vanilla Smoothie – frozen cherries, raspberries, vanilla yogurt and milk

- Creamy Coffee Smoothie – instant coffee, sugar and cream or ice cream

TAKE A MOMENT TO PLAY AGAIN

The great man is he who does not lose his child's-heart.

— Mencius, Book IV

- Play some children's games: hopscotch, hide and seek, rope-skipping games
- Build sand castles on the beach
- Fly a kite
- Draw with crayons
- Read a good children's book, or some old childhood favourites
- Watch a children's movie
- Read a joke book, tell some silly jokes
- Spend some time in a candy store
- Make some paper airplanes. Fly them

FUN DATES

- Plan a surprise lunchtime picnic
- Drive along the outer borders of your city or county, exploring new neighbourhoods and villages where you've never been
- Take a walk in the rain
- Go fly a kite - seriously! Go on a picnic followed by kite flying on a windy day
- Explore a wild and scenic place you've always wanted to check out
- Ride a city's entire public rail transit system, going out on remote branch lines, just for the fun of it
- Go up to the top of a building in the city
- Test drive a sports car together
- Take a rowboat out on a lake at sunset
- Hike to the top of a mountain for a picnic

WAYS TO CULTIVATE
TRUE BEAUTY

Beauty is God's handwriting.
Welcome it in every fair face,
every fair day, every fair flower.

– Charles Kingsley

- Think of someone who is hurting that you can reach out to today, offering your kindness and compassion

- Ask God to help you not to respond in anger when someone wrongs you

- Make a point of it to focus on others when you are with them, at making them feel appreciated

- Make a decision not to compare yourself with others

- Be positive and cheerful when you are with others

GARDENING IDEAS FOR SPRING TIME

There can be no other occupation like gardening in which, if you were to creep up behind someone at their work, you would find them smiling.

– Mirabel Osler

- Plant a vegetable garden: Include spinach, beetroot, lettuce, bush beans, eggplant, chillies, summer cabbage, radishes and leeks

- Create a butterfly corner: Butterflies are easily attracted. Plant their favourite flowers in a protected yet sunny spot. Flowers to include are impatiens, marigold, zinnia, cosmos, butterfly weed, purple coneflower, black-eyed Susan and bee balm. Chillies also make beautiful pot plants

- Plant some veggies in pots: Peppers, chillies, tomatoes, peas and beans look beautiful and provide something for your table. Add some herbs too

- Create beautiful flowerboxes: combine flowering plants of bright colours with some leafy foliage plants; mix a variety of shapes together or play with combinations or complementary colours

LOVING OTHERS

... And the second is like it:
'Love your neighbour as yourself.'

– Matthew 22:37–39

- Make a list of practical acts of kindness you can do for others, and start working on your list throughout the following weeks

- Make a point of telling your family that you love them

- Ask God to help you show patience instead of anger when an employee (or family member!) makes a mistake

- Set aside time for the people you care about

SPRINGCLEAN YOUR LIFE

Your outer world is a reflection of your inner world. If you change your thinking, you change your life.

– Brian Tracy

- Clean out the anger, hatred, jealousy, and self doubt and make some room for happiness and positive thoughts

- Wash away delay and procrastination

- Dust off your attitude, and put on a fresh coat of positive living

- Throw out misunderstanding, and lack of patience; sweep out the dirt of gossip or lies; open the shades and let in the warmth of friendship

- Lighten up your thoughts with humour and fun

- Open the windows of your mind to new ideas and a fresh perspective on living a happier, better, easier life

ACCESSORIES TO STIR THE SPRING FEELING

If honor be your clothing, the suit will last a lifetime; but if clothing be your honor, it will soon be worn threadbare.

– William Arnot

- A new pair of pretty earrings in spring colours
- Bright and happy flip flops
- An elegant watch matching your personality and style
- Bright and trendy cell phone covers
- Invest in a stylish dress for formal functions

SPRING IDEAS FOR YOUR HOME

*Plant your own garden and decorate your own soul,
instead of waiting for someone to bring you flowers.*

– Veronica A Shoffstall

- ❧ Spring is the perfect time to bring a color into your home that you've never used there before. Keep spring and summer colors and accessories light, both in feel and color

- ❧ If your furniture is centered in front of a fireplace, think about ways to rearrange the look for summer. Change the focal point away from the mantel to a view of a garden

- ❧ Change dark-patterned decorative pillows by covering them with fresh, floral prints or plaids for warmer weather

- ❧ Have your draperies made so they are reversible, allowing you to easily turn them from lively to neutral with the seasonal changes

- ❧ Be sure to put garden magazines and flower books out on the coffee table in the spring and summer

- ❧ Add brightly colored vases, spunky patterned pillows, a painted jute rug, and flea market finds to your space for a fresh feel without spending a fortune

- ❧ Remove old and tired table linens and winter accessories, and opt for pastel colors and lively spring patterns

- Bring out a simple bowl and display your fruits, and even your vegetables

- Clear most of the artwork and accessories out of your room, and just keep a few larger, simpler pieces

- Use your glassware as vases, pencil holders, or candy dishes – glass sparkles and adds a bit of sunshine to a room

- Add white! White with your present color scheme will both cool and brighten, adding the freshness that only white can

- Put out candles in shades of violet, yellow, pink, and green

- Change bathroom towels to lighter coordinating shades

- Use flowers as centerpieces, on the countertop in an old porcelain pitcher, in a vase in the bathroom or on an occasional table

- Clean out your fireplace and fill it with a display of varying heights of candles, a floral arrangement, or white birch logs stacked neatly

- Take down heavy drapes, and replace with sheers or unlined curtains

- Remove thick and dark-coloured rugs and replace them with natural fibre rugs

SEVEN SPRING-CLEANING TIPS FOR THE WORKPLACE

*Choose a job you love,
and you will never have to work
a day in your life.*

– Confucius

- Have a thorough desk/file clear out – it will focus you and ease stress
- Handle every piece of paper and e-mail once wherever possible
- Arrive and leave on time – it sounds simple – make it a habit
- Start and end the day with a clear desk – this reduces 'back to work phobia'
- Go out of the office at lunch to ensure you take a break – more productive, less stress
- Regularly schedule time in your diary for your family, friends, interests and holidays
- Avoid squabbles/personality clashes – focus on your priorities

RECONNECT

Letters are among the most significant memorial a person can leave behind them.

– Johann Wolfgang von Goethe

- Set a coffee date with a friend you have not seen for the past month

- Each evening this week phone one person you have not spoken to for a while

- SMS five people to encourage them and let them know you are thinking of them

- Update your birthday list and make a special effort to contact everyone when it's their birthday

- E-mail a picture of you and your family to your friends with a quick update on what you've been up to

MAKE YOUR OWN LISTS

If you aim at nothing, you'll hit it every time.

– Author Unknown

- Places to see before I turn forty/fifty/sixty
- Ten ways to spoil my grandchildren
- Challenges to tackle before my next birthday
- Things to learn in the next six months
- Must-see movies
- Friends I want to look up in the next year
- Fears I want to overcome
- Words I need to say to people before …
- Five surprises I want to give my husband
- ....
- ....
- ....
- ....

QUOTES TO
CELEBRATE SPRING

The day the Lord created hope was probably
the same day he created Spring.

– Bern Williams

❧

Hope is like a bird that senses dawn and
carefully starts to sing while it is still dark.

– Author unknown

❧

Those who bring sunshine into the lives of others
cannot keep it from themselves.

– Sir James M Barrie

❧

No winter lasts forever;
no spring skips its turn.

– Hal Borland

The world is full of suffering,
it is also full of overcoming it.

– Helen Keller

᭝

An optimist is the human personification of spring.

– Susan J Bissonette

᭝

There is something infinitely healing in the repeated
refrains of nature – the assurance that dawn comes
after night, and spring after winter.

– Rachel Carson

᭝

Love comes to those who still hope even though
they've been disappointed, to those who still believe
even though they've been betrayed, to those who still
love even though they've been hurt before.

᭝

Happiness is like a butterfly which, when pursued,
is always beyond our grasp, but, if you will sit
down quietly, may alight upon you.

– Nathaniel Hawthorne

VERSES FILLED WITH THE JOY OF SPRING

You turned my wailing into dancing;
you removed my sackcloth
and clothed me with joy ...

– Psalm 30:11

See! The winter is past; the rains are over and gone.
Flowers appear on the earth; the season of singing
has come, the cooing of doves is heard in our land.
The fig tree forms its early fruit; the blossoming
vines spread their fragrance. Arise, come, my
darling; my beautiful one, come with me.

– Song of Solomon 2:11–13

May the God of hope fill you with all
joy and peace as you trust in him,
so that you may overflow with hope
by the power of the Holy Spirit.

– Romans 15:13

Jesus said to her, 'I am the resurrection
and the life. He who believes in me will live,
even though he dies; and whoever lives
and believes in me will never die.'

– John 11:25–26

May the God of hope fill you with all
joy and peace as you trust in him,
so that you may overflow with hope
by the power of the Holy Spirit.

– Romans 15:13

Blessed be the God and Father of our Lord Jesus
Christ! By his great mercy he has given us
a new birth into a living hope through the
resurrection of Jesus Christ from the dead ..

– 1 Peter 1:3

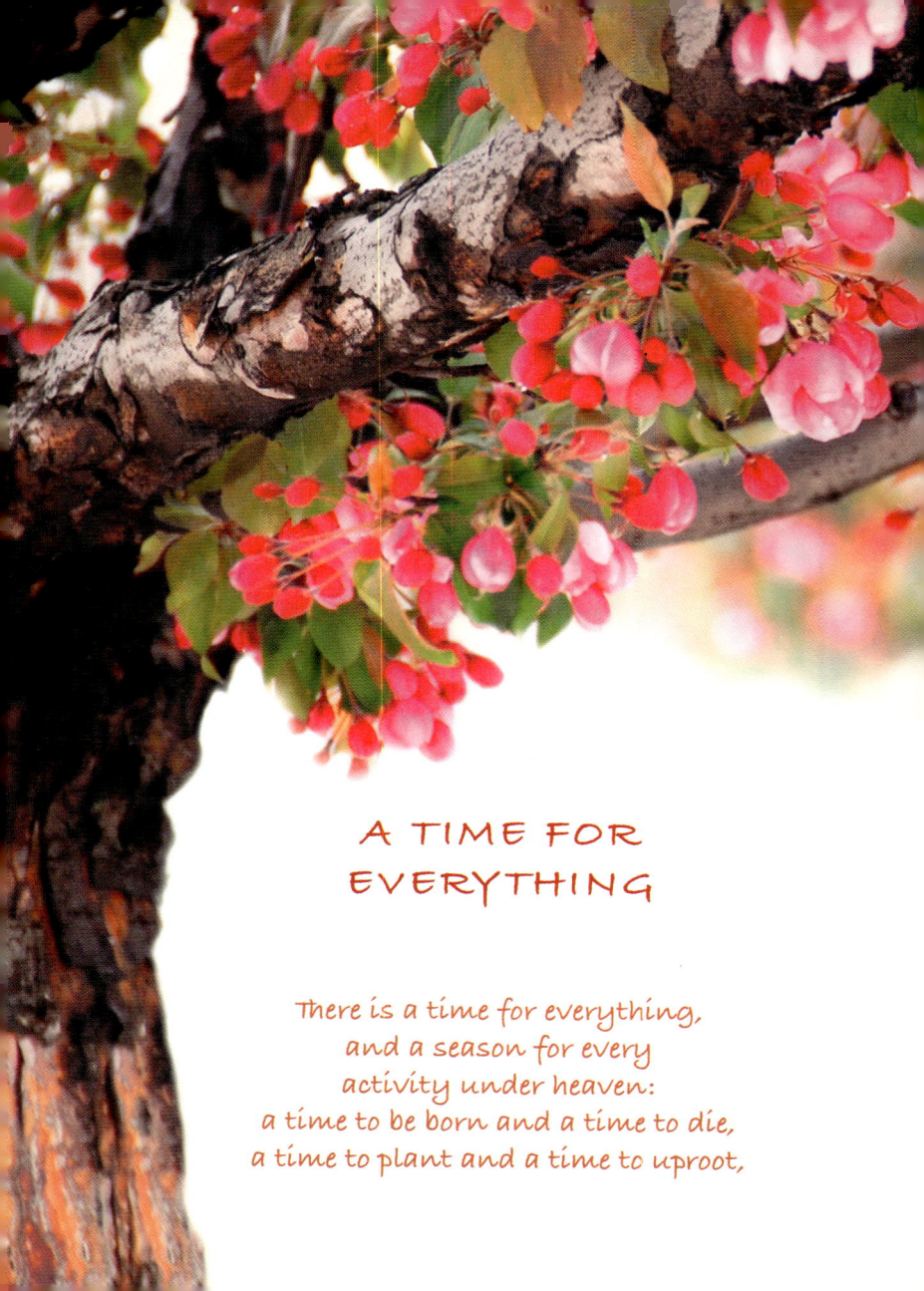

A TIME FOR EVERYTHING

There is a time for everything,
and a season for every
activity under heaven:
a time to be born and a time to die,
a time to plant and a time to uproot,

a time to kill and a time to heal,
a time to tear down and a time to build,
a time to weep and a time to laugh,
a time to mourn and a time to dance,
a time to scatter stones and a time to gather them,
a time to embrace and a time to refrain,
a time to search and a time to give up,
a time to keep and a time to throw away,
a time to tear and a time to mend,
a time to be silent and a time to speak,
a time to love and a time to hate,
a time for war and a time for peace.

– Ecclesiastes 3:1–8

B•I•B•L•O•G•R•A•P•H•Y

Gray, S. *Destitute Gourmet* (Struik Publishers, Cape Town: 2004)
(p 100, 102)

Hudson, T. *The Serenity Prayer* (Struik Christian Books, Cape Town:
2002) (p 18, 46)

Keys, J. *Live Your Dream* (Struik Christian Books, Cape Town: 2006)
(p 84, 105)

Wales, S. *The Art of Romantic Living* (Thomas Nelson Publishers,
Nashvill, Tennessee: 2003) (p 28)

Many websites served as inspiration and a lot of the ideas have been
gleaned from the internet. Substantial parts of particular lists have
been taken from the following sites:

http://www.discoverfun.com/freeinfo/500fun/index.html (used in
many of the 'things to do' lists)

http://www.smallstep.gov/sm steps/sm steps index.html (used in many
lists on health and fitness)

http://www.wikihow.com/Be-Confident (p 14)

http://www.wikihow.com/Be-Yourself (p 36)

http://www.eioba.com/a79827/simple_living_manifesto_72_ideas_to_
simplify_your_life (p 42)

http://www.recipegoldmine.com/articles/makingyourown.html (p 70)

http://www.inspiration-for-singles.com/lighten-your-load.html (109)

http://ezinearticles.com/?Top-10-Best-Smoothie-Recipes&id=448954
(p 112)

Flower box5 Steps to Beautiful Flowerboxes (p 116)

http://www.flowerframers.com/flowerboxeshelpfultips.htm (p 116)

http://www.lifeorganizers.com/spirit-mind/clean-your-life.htm (p 118)

http://nuyu-life-coaching.co.uk/41/life-spring-cleaning-tips/ (p 122)

http://interiordec.about.com/od/springdecor/tp/top_summerdec.htm (120)

http://interiordec.about.com/cs/seasonaldecor/ht/ht_changeseason.htm
(p 120)

We would like to hear from you.
Please send your comments about this book to us at:
reviews@struikchristianbooks.co.za

STRUIK CHRISTIAN GIFTS
www.struikchristianbooks.co.za